Revelation for Laymen

By: Dr. Larry G Morgan

Self-Published by Larry Morgan, 6665 N NC Hwy 109, Winston-Salem, NC
27107   336-769-2210

ISBN-978-1796593945

Front Cover Artwork:

https://upload.wikimedia.org/wikipedia/commons/7/79/BambergA
pocalypseFolio019v7AngelsWith7TrumpetsAnd1WithCenser.JPG

Dedication

This book is dedicated to my granddaughter, Melanie, who helped me with the manuscript.

Prologue

A book about the Bible is about the last kind of book I ever thought I'd write. And the last book of the Bible I thought I'd write about is the book Revelation. Most people feel like the book of Revelation is too full of symbols and symbolism to be adequately understood. I was of this opinion also. After reading the book, I decided that it would be helpful to the average person if a shorter version of the most important verses and actions were created. That is what I have tried to do in Revelation for Laymen. I have made extensive use of references to interpret the scripture as well as some of my own input. As a result, I believe I have a book that the average Bible scholar will find interesting and useful. At least, some of my friends who are ministers have said it is so.

I hope you find my book both interesting and helpful as you study Revelation.

Dr. Larry G. Morgan

Table of Contents

Preface

The undisputed author of the book of Revelation is John the Apostle. He is also the same John who was one of Jesus's disciples. He was the youngest of the disciples being only about eighteen years old at the time of Jesus's ministry. John is also the author of the Gospel of John, having written it around A.D 85. Obviously, he was an old man in his late eighties or nineties. It is believed that he was one of Jesus's closest friends and advisors. He is also the person that Jesus, as he hung on the cross, asked to take his mother, Mary, and care for her. John was the last of the disciples, and was the only one to die a natural death, all of the others it is believed died a violent death as a result of their preaching the gospel.

John was the pastor of the church at Ephesus, and was the "overseer" of several other churches in that province of the Roman Empire. About A.D. 95, he was arrested by the Romans for reaching the gospel and sent to the isle of Patmos where he was to spend the next ten years of his life in exile before being released. Patmos is a ten miles long and five miles wide island in the eastern Agean Sea just off of the coast of what is the nation of Turkey today. In John's day, the area was known as Asia, but it, of course, was not the continent of Asia. It later became known as Asia Minor. It was there about this time that John, sometimes referred to as John the Revelator, wrote the Book of Revelation.

The Book of Revelation is made up of six basic parts. Chapter 1 is basically the introduction and greetings. Chapter 2 begins with the letters to the seven churches in Asia Minor. Next is the opening of the Seven Seals. This is followed by the blowing of the seven trumpets. Then comes the pouring out of the seven vials or bowls of wrath. The last part covers the time period from the last of the vials to the end of the Millennial Reign. Interspersed between the opening of the sixth and eventh seals is a brief interlude as well as between the blowing of the sixth and seven trumpets. These interludes basically cover the religious and political develops during the seven years of tribulation.

For the first verses of Revelation I will give only a brief glance as they deal with subjects such as Verse 1, the title of the book and the steps of the Revelation which are from top to bottom, God the Father downward to Jesus Christ who hands it to the angel who will carry the revelation to John who will make it available to the servants such as us today. Verse 2 gives us the method of revelation. Verse 3 is a beatitude for those who read the epistle and hear it. Verses 4, 5, and 6 are the greetings from John and Christ in heaven. Verses 7 and 8 describe His second coming and clearly identifies himself as Alpha and Omega, the beginning and the ending. Verse 9 shows the post-incarnate Christ in a glorified body judging His church. (At this time the church has been raptured, but the Old Testament saints and the Tribulation saints will not be resurrected until the end of the seven year period of Tribulation and the Great Tribulation.)

Note that the title of this work is Revelation for Laymen. I have not recorded every verse and tried to expound on it. I have tried to pick out the most prominent verses that provoke the most interest and comment and still preserve the overall message of the book. There are several interpretations of almost every point in Revelation, so I have tried to present the clearest one to me.

The Beginning

"I was in the spirit on the Lord's Day and heard behind me a great voice as of a trumpet,

Saying I am Alpha and Omega, the first and the last: and, What thou seest, write in a book, and send it to the seven churches in Asia...." {Rev. 1:10-11}

And I turned to see the voice that spake with me. And being turned, I saw seven golden candlesticks; And in the midst of the seven candlesticks one like unto the Son of man, clothed with a garment down to the foot, and girt about the paps with a golden girdle." {Rev. 12: 12-13}

These seven candlesticks (or lampstands) represent the seven churches in Asia. Jesus is here pictured as the High Priest. His garment represents the righteousness of Christ.

"His head and his hair were white like wool, as white as snow; and his eyes were as a flame of fire;

And his feet like unto fine brass, as if they burned in a furnace; and his voice as the sound of many waters." {Rev. 1:14-15}

His hair speaks of his eternal existence and his eyes of his penetrating insight. His feet of brass are symbolic of judgement. His voice as the sound of many waters is the voice of authority.

"And he had in his right hand seven stars: and out of his mouth a two-edge sword: and his countenance was as the sun shineth in his strength." {Rev. 1: 16}

Jesus himself reveals to us the meaning of the stars and candlesticks.

"The mystery of the seven stars which thou sawest in my right hand, and the seven golden candlesticks. The seven stars are the angels of the seven churches: and the seven candlesticks which thou sawest are the seven churches." {Rev. 1: 20}

This is self-explanatory except for the seven angels. They usually refer to messengers, but here they probably are the seven pastors of the seven churches in Asia.

Letters to the Seven Churches in Asia

Chapter 2 and 3 are mostly the letters to the seven churches in Asia Minor from God to Jesus to the angel to John to us.

"John to the seven churches which are in Asia: Grace be unto you, and peace, from him which is, which was, and which is to come: and from the seven Spirits which are before his throne" {Rev. 1: 4} This is a wonderful greeting from John. The seven spirits represents completeness. The people of John's day was well aware of its significance.

"I am Alpha and Omega, the beginning and the ending, saith the Lord, which is, which was, and which is to come, the Almighty" {Rev.1: 8}

Now we begin the examination of the second main section of the book, the letters to the seven churches of Asia Minor. These include Ephesus,

Smyrna, Pergamum, Thyatira, Sardis, Philadelphia
and Laodicea. There are great differences of
opinion of the dates and time periods for each of
the church ages by expositors of Revelation.
The letters open with commendations to the
churches. After the commendations, John lists
some condemnations of the churches.

Christ's Letter to the Church in Ephesus
"Unto the angel of the church of Ephesus write;
these things saith he that holdeth the seven stars in
his right hand, who walketh in the midst of the
seven golden candle sticks." {Rev. 2:1}
This refers to a vision John saw in heaven of Jesus
walking among seven golden candlesticks, Verses
12 and 13. The seven golden candlesticks
represent the seven churches in Asia to whom the
letters will go, and the seven stars indicate that He
holds and controls the universe. However, they
could represent the seven pastors, or overseers, of
the seven churches.

First come the commendations.

"I know thy works, and thy labor, and thy patience, and how thou canst not bear them which are evil: and thou hast tried them which say they are apostles, and are not, and hast found them liars: And hast borne, and hast patience, and for my name's sake hast labored, and hast not fainted." (given up) {Rev. 2: 2-3}

Later on He commends them further "…..thou hast hated the deeds of the Nicolaitans which I also hate." {Rev. 2: 6}

The Nicolaitans were a cult which taught that one must indulge in sin to understand it.

Here we need to understand that He is speaking to believers because Jesus does not ask the lost world for good works. He commends this church for their weariness in their labor for Him. Next the Lord Jesus commended them for testing men whether or not they were really apostles, and if they were not, asked them to leave town. (The main requirement for an apostle was one had to have seen the risen Lord.) He commends them for bearing the cross and preaching Christ and having not grown weary. These commendations also apply to the period of church history between Pentecost and A.D. 100, which the Ephesian church represents. It is known as the Apostolic Church.

Next come the condemnations.

"Nevertheless I have some what against thee, because thou hast left thy first love." {Rev.2:4} They had lost their enthusiastic and burning intensity for the person of Christ. Ephesus had many attractions that were beginning to draw the believers away from their first love for Jesus Christ. Ephesus was a large cosmopolitan city with many attractions that could draw the Christians astray.

Jesus's answer to them is seen in Rev. 2; 5.

"Remember therefore from whence thou are fallen, and repent, and do the first works; or else I will come unto thee quickly, and will remove thy candlestick out of his place, except thou repent." By removal of their candlestick is meant that they would lose the effectiveness of their witness to the lost world for Christ. As one pastor phrased it, God would put them on the "shelf of do nothing."

Christ's Letter to the Church in Smyrna

Smyrna represents the martyr church which covers the period from approximately A.D. 100 to A.D. 314, from the death of the Apostle John to the Edict of Toleration by Constantine in A. D. 313 and ended the persecution of the Christians all over the Roman Empire. This is one of two churches that Christ, through John, did not list any condemnations.

"And unto the angel (pastor, overseer) of the church in Smyrna write: These things sayeth the first and the last, which was dead, and is alive (Jesus)." {Rev. 2:8}

"Fear none of these things which thou shall suffer: behold, the devil shall cast some of you into prison, that ye may be tried; and ye shall have tribulation ten days: be thou faithful unto death, and I will give thee a crown of life." {Rev. 2: 9-10}

 The devil was going to cast some of them into prison. Many would lose their lives.

"Ye shall have tribulation "ten days." {Rev. 2: 9-10}

This refers to ten intense periods of persecution by ten different emperors, beginning with Nero in A.D. 64 through Diocletian in A.D. 313. It is reliably reported that Nero had Christians soaked in wax, or other combustible material, and hung in his garden. Then they were set on fire to give light for him and his guests when they had parties.

"Be thou faithful unto death and I will give thee a crown of life," {Rev. 2: 10}

Crowns that will be eternal. And they were faithful. They were martyrs for Him.

The church at Smyrna is the church during the terrible era of Christians being fed to the lions and other wild beasts in the coliseums, especially the Roman coliseum. They were covered with the fresh skins of sheep and turned into the coliseum and wild, starved-crazed dogs attacked them and killed them savagely. These victims included little children. They were also given swords and lances and ordered to fight until one of them killed the other. This was great entertainment for the Romans of that time.

Christ's Letter to the Church in Pergamum
The church in Pergamum represents the church during the period of approximately A.D. 314 to A.D. 590. This is basically when the Roman Empire disappeared in Western Europe, yet it continued in the Middle East as the Byzantine Empire until around 1350.
It was a time when paganism entered the church and the church began to move away from the

person of Christ. These included such things as ancestor worship, praying for the dead, and worship of holy relics all of which pre-date the coming of Christ. For example, people have worshiped and venerated such things as a piece of wood purported to have been a piece of the cross. They had permitted two doctrines of error to penetrate their worship, which God held against them: the doctrine of Balaam and the doctrine of the Nicolaitans. The error of the Nicolaitans is not exactly known, but it probably had something to do with introduction of pagan ritualism by the clergy into the church. The error of Balaam was the teaching that it was alright to eat things sacrificed to idols and to commit fornication. He taught that the way to corrupt Israel was by intermarriage with Moabite women. And during the period that the church at Pergamum represents, the unconverted world came into the church. In Rev. 2:16, the church is exhorted to "Repent; or else I will come quickly and will fight against them with the sword of my mouth." (His spoken word).

Christ's Letter to the Church in Thyatira

The church at Thyatira represents the church from A.D. 590 to approximately A.D. 1000. (Some Bible historians set the upper limit at A.D. 1500.) It is representative of Romanism, and it was a dark period. Today this period in history is called the Dark Ages. It was a time when pagan practices and idolatry were mingled with Christian works and worship including such things as praying for the dead, burning candles, kissing the Pope's foot, worshiping of images and saints and angels and relics, and so forth.

The church at Thyatira was commended for its charity, and service, and patience, and works. They are condemned because they had allowed a woman whose counterpart was Jezebel of the Old Testament to teach and seduce some of them to commit fornication and to eat things sacrificed to idols. It was during the latter years of this period that the Inquisition was introduced into the Church which resulted in literally hundreds of thousands of men and women being put to death, mostly being burned alive, because of being suspected of heresy and other spurious accusations against the Catholic Church. These were the years when the Church dominated the serfs and held them in subjection to the whims of the Church. They had to pay high church taxes and were even charged fees to have the church clergy pray their relatives out of purgatory, an accepted church doctrine that was introduced into the church during these years. These were the years of the great church-sponsored crusades from approximately A.D. 1096 to A.D. 1250. Corruption was rampant in the church, especially in the latter years of this era.

Christ's Letter to the Church in Sardis
Sardis represents the church during the period from A.D. 1517 through A.D. 1800. This is the era of the Protestant church. It began when the

Great Reformation began ignited by Martin Luther and takes us through the great missionary movement in the history of the church. This is the church that recovered the doctrine of justification by faith and is commended for that. However, God had some condemnation for this church because of the emphasis they put on works. However, he did commend them because this faith in works had resulted in good works.

"And unto the angel of the church in Sardis write: These things saith he that hath the seven spirits of God, and the seven stars; (Jesus) I know thy works, and thou hast a name that thou livest, and art dead."

The Protestant churches at that time as a whole were just going through the motions of worship. They were building all the time and people were coming on Sunday morning but did not have enough of the Spirit to come back on Sunday and Wednesday nights. They are just going through the motions.

He also commends them for having a remnant who are faithful.

"Thou hast a few names even in Sardis which have not defiled their garments; they shall walk with me in white: for they are worthy." {Rev. 3: 4}

Christ's Letter to the Church in Philadelphia
The church in Philadelphia represents the revived church dating from A.D. 1800 to the Rapture. Obviously it is the present-day church. It is commended for having turned back to the Word of God. People are wanting to hear the Word of God today. This is the second church for which there are no condemnations. It did not get its name from the Bible but rather it got it because of the love Attalus II had for his brother, Eumenes, who was king of Pergamum. Hence the city of brotherly love.

"I know thy works: behold, I have set before thee and open door, and no man can shut it: for thou hast a little strength, and hast kept my word, and hast not denied my name. {Rev. 3: 8}.

Christ's Letter to the Church in Laodicea

This is the only church that God has no commendations for.

"I know thy works, that thou art neither hot nor cold: I would thou wert cold or hot. So then because thou art neither cold nor hot, I will spue thee out of my mouth." Rev. 3:15-16}

The Loadicean church and the Philadelphia church are existing together at the same time today, according to many theologians. However, some theologians insist the church of Philadelphia ends at 1900 and the Laodicean church begins at 1900 and continues to the Rapture. I'm not sure I believe this, but I can see evidences of the practices of Laodicea beginning to occur today. This great split consists of those who believe and hear the Word of God and follow it, and love it, and those that reject it. "Because thou sayest, I am rich, and increased with goods, and have need of nothing; and knowest not that thou are wretched, and miserable, and poor, and blind and naked." {Rev. 3: 17}

It is the remnants of this Laodicean church that will be left behind at the Rapture and will go into the Tribulation period as the Apostate church. During the age of these two church periods, the Rapture of the church occurs and the church is taken up to meet the Lord in the air. This marks the beginning of the tribulation period of seven years.

This also ends the era of the seven churches. Some expositors believe that each church has a few representatives of all the others in it existing at the same time. I believe there is some overlapping, but by and large, I believe that most of the church ages reflect the one kind of church identified with it.

The Church in Heaven with Christ

"And immediately I was in the spirit; and behold, a throne was set in heaven, and one sat on the throne." [Rev. 4: 2}

"And around about the throne were four and twenty seats: and upon the seats I saw four and twenty elders sitting, clothed in white raiment; and they had on their heads crowns of gold." {Rev. 4: 4}

These elders are representative of the total church from Pentecost to the Rapture.

"And before the throne there was a sea of glass like unto crystal: and in the midst of the throne, and round about the throne, were four beasts (better translated as living creatures) full of eyes before and behind. {Rev. 4: 6}

And the first beast was like a lion, and the second beast like a calf, and the third beast had the face of a man, and the fourth beast was like a flying eagle." {Rev. 4: 7}

The first creature represents Christ as a king, the second creature represents Christ as a servant, the third as the Son sf Man, and the fourth represents the deity of Christ.

"And the four beasts had each of them six wings about him; and they were full of eyes within: and they rest not day and night, saying, Holy, holy, holy, Lord God Almighty, which was, and is, and is to come."

The six wings correspond to the seraphim of Isaiah 6: 2 which are also repeating the refrain of holy, holy, holy Lord God Almighty. The eyes means that Jesus sees all that man does, good and bad.

Chapter 5 is a continuing of Chapter 4 which the reader needs to review on his own. This is the place where the little book is found and only Christ is worthy to open it. It is the book that contains the seven seals which are to be examined next. John weeps because this scroll is the title deed to the earth and that as long it is kept sealed, Satan will be in charge of the earth.

Reasons for the Seven Year Period of Tribulations

(1) To finish the transgression of Israel. The rebellions against the leadership of God of Israel will be finished.

(2) To put an end to sin. What will it be like to live in a perfect world without sin!

(3) To atone for wickedness. The wicked will get what is due them for all the terrible crimes they have done to their fellowmen like killing babies and other heinous crimes. The seals, trumpets, and vials will provide much punishment for crimes against the righteous during the seven years of the Tribulation and Great Tribulation, especially for the saints under the altar in heaven.

(4) To bring in everlasting righteousness for mankind. This is something he has not had since the Garden of Eden.

(5) To seal up vision and prophesy. There will be no more need for vision and prophesy. It will all have been fulfilled.

 I always look for the reasons for why things happen, and I believe these are good reasons for the seven years of tribulations.

The Beginning of Tribulation

 Note: "Tribulation" refers to the first half, 42 months, of the seven year period and "Great Tribulation" refers to the second half, 42 months, of the seven year period.

Opening of the Seven Seals

"And I saw when the lamb opened one of the seals, as it were the noise of thunder, one of the four beasts (living creatures sitting around God's throne in heaven), saying, Come and see."

Opening of the First Seal

"And I saw and behold a white horse: and he that sat him had a bow; and a crown was given unto him: and he went forth conquering, and to conquer." {Rev. 6: 12-2}

Most expositors agree that the rider of this white horse is none other than the Antichrist. (Some expositors identify him as Christ himself.) This indicates the beginning of the Antichrist's attempt to take over the political government and apostate church. The fact that he has a bow and no arrow indicates that he is going to conquer by diplomacy rather than by force. This angel enables the Antichrist to establish a short, temporary period of peace on the earth, especially for Israel. Israel will be assured of peace and safety from the other nations, but it will only last three and one half years.

Opening of the Second Seal

"And when he had opened the second seal, I heard the second beast (from around the throne in heaven) say, Come and see. And there went out another horse that was red: and power was given to him that sat thereon to take peace from the earth, and that they should kill one another: And there was given to him a great sword." {Rev. 6 3-4} Following is partially conjecture on my part. The Antichrist, with the aid of the False Prophet, will sign a peace treaty with Israel, you recall, that he will break it at the end of the first three and half years, and try to take over rule of the entire world. This war begins because several of the nations rebel at this attempt by the Antichrist and world war breaks out and millions die. Where is the United States while all of this is going on? Apparently the western nations will not have a part in these proceedings and events. There is some scripture which mentions that "fire will rain on the isles and coastlands." Some expositors have speculated that these isles and coastlands refer to the United States and other western nations. (If my memory serves me correctly, this information comes from Hal Lindsey's little book, "The Late Great Planet Earth"). Some commentators believe the United States may be unable to participate in these events due to an earlier war when Russia (Gog and Magog) came down to try to destroy Israel. But they are supernaturally destroyed by Christ. Russia will be allied with the Arab nations in this attempt to destroy Israel. (We are told that it will take the people of Israel seven years to locate and burn the implements of war after this conflict is ended which indicates the presence of radio activity. This means this could be a nuclear war and the United States is reeling or destroyed from an atomic attack.) This occurs near the beginning of the Tribulation or, perhaps, just before the beginning of the Tribulation. (Ezekiel 38-39) Anyway, it seems the United States will not have a major part in these end time events.

The only role I can possibly see for the United States is that it is one of the nations of the world who rebel against the efforts of Antichrist to rule the world and gets involved in that war. The armies of Antichrist win this war and he becomes the one world ruler.

Opening of the Third Seal—Rider on a Black Horse

"And when he had opened the third seal, I heard the beast say, Come and see. And I beheld, and lo a black horse; and he that sat on him had a pair of balances in his hand."

"And I heard a voice in the midst of the four beasts say, A measure of wheat for a penny, and three measures of barley for a penny; and see thou hurt not the oil and the wine." {Rev. 6: 5—6}

The color of the black horse speaks of mourning and famine. Famine always occurs after a war which causes much mourning. The above verse indicates the shortage of food stuffs at this time all over the world and the impossible high prices for food. It will take a day's wages to purchase one quart of barley. This is what it takes to feed one man per day, so there will be nothing left for his family. The oil and wine are luxuries enjoyed by the wealthy and they will still be able to get them. This is almost always true during wartime.

Opening of the Fourth Seal—Rider on a Pale Horse

"And when he had opened the fourth seal. I heard the voice of the fourth beast saying, Come up hither.

And I looked and behold a pale horse and his name that sat on him was Death, and Hell followed with him. And power was given unto them over the fourth part of the earth, to kill with a sword, and with hunger, and with death, and with the beasts of the earth." {Rev. 6—8}

The rider's name is death, and the pestilence is a disease, or diseases, that will kill one fourth of the world's population. It seems that the beasts of the earth-lions and tigers and dogs, etc. will turn on mankind at this time as well.

Opening of the Fifth Seal—Prayer of the Martyred Remnant

"And when he had opened the fifth seal. I saw under the alter (near God's throne in heaven) the souls of them that were slain for the word of God, and for the testimony which they held,
And they cried with a loud voice, saying, How long, O Lord, holy and true, dost thou not judge and avenge our blood on them that dwell on earth?" {Rev. 6: 9—10}
This alter is in heaven and where Christ offered His blood for the sins of the world. The souls under the altar are Old Testament saints. Included with these are those who will be slain during the Great Tribulation period, I believe. Anyway, their white robes give special status in heaven. On earth during the first part of the seven year period, the

Tribulation, it will be time of the greatest persecution of Christians in history. Many will be killed for their witness.

"And white robes were given unto every one of them; and it was said unto them. That they should rest yet a little season, until their fellow servants also and their brethren, that should be killed as they were, should be fulfilled."{Rev. 6: 11} This means the Tribulation saints are in the second resurrection along with the Old Testament saints. This is my interruption of this verse, and I hope I have done it correctly. (It is difficult to distinguish the different resurrections from my various sources.)

Opening of the Sixth Seal---The Day of Wrath Has Come

"And I beheld when he had opened the sixth seal, and, lo, there was a great earthquake and the sun became black as sackcloth, and the moon became as blood;

And the stars of heaven fell unto the earth, even as a fig tree casteth her untimely figs, when she is shaken of a mighty wind." {Rev. 6: 12-13}

These are believed to be meteorites.

This is the beginning of the last half of the Great Tribulation which last three and a half years. Half of this is 42 months. The great day of his wrath has come. The stars falling from heaven are probably symbolic.

"And the heaven departed as a scroll when it is rolled together; and every mountain and island was move out of their places." {Rev. 6:14}

"And the kings of the earth and the great men, and the rich men, and the chief captains, and the mighty men, and every bondman, and every freeman, hid themselves in the dens and in the rocks of the mountains;

And said to the mountains and rocks, Fall on us, and hide us from the face of him that sitteth on the throne, and from the wrath of the Lamb." {Rev. 6: 15}

These verses should be taken literally and are self-explanatory. Everyone recognizes that Jesus is the cause of this calamity and judgment.

It should be noted that the opening of the seven seals cover the first twenty-one months of the Tribulation. The seven trumpet judgments cover the second quarter, or the second twenty-one months of the Tribulation.

Interlude between Sixth and Seventh Seals

Now we come to an interlude between the sixth seal and the seventh seal. The reason is given in the first three verses of this chapter, chapter seven as follows.

"And after these things I saw four angels standing on the four corners of the earth, holding the four winds of the earth, that the wind shall not blow on the earth, nor on the sea, nor on any tree." {Rev. 7:1}

"After these things…" refers to the judgments of the previous chapter.

"And I saw another angel ascending from the east, having the seal of the living God: and he cried with a loud voice to the four angels, to whom it was given to hurt the earth and the sea,

Saying, Hurt not the earth, neither the sea, nor the trees, till we and sealed the servants of our God in their foreheads." Rev. 7: 2—3}

The people who do not take the seal of the Antichrist, the mark of the beast, are also given a seal in their foreheads to identify and secure them during the Tribulation, to shield them from some of the plagues during this time. However, the Bible doesn't say what the seal is, and there is much disagreement about it. At least one expositor says that it is to be taken spiritually. He believes the mark will be in their lives:…By their fruits ye shall know them." Matt. 7:20 Their separated, Godly lives are going to be the mark and what sets them apart.

What this seal was, how it looked is not described. Later there will be a multitude of Gentiles saved also, too many to count. In fact there will be more people saved during the Tribulation and Great Tribulation than in the previous Old Testament years and the Church Age together.

"After this I beheld, and, lo, a great multitude , which no man can number, of all nations, and kindreds, and people, and tongues, stood before the throne, and before the Lamb, clothed with white robes, and palms in their hands;

And cried with a loud voice, saying, Salvation to our God which sitteth upon the throne, and unto the Lamb." {Rev. 7: 9—10}

At this point in the scripture there is some overlapping and it is difficult to keep the multitudes of Gentiles separate from the one hundred and forty-four thousand Jews that will become flaming evangelists during this tribulation period.

Now we come to the remnant of Israel that will be saved during this seven year period. This means that these one hundred and forty-four thousand

Jews are going to preach the gospel during the Tribulation which is the first half of the seven year period, and multitudes of gentiles are going to be saved.

"And I heard the number of them which were sealed: and there were sealed an hundred and forty-four thousand of all of the children of Israel." Rev. 7:4}

This one hundred and forty-four thousand, twelve thousand from each of the twelve tribes, represents the remnant of Israel that God preserves down through the centuries. These are flaming evangelists on the order of Paul the Apostle who carry the gospel to the entire world during this seven year period.

This saving of the one hundred and forty-four thousand and the resultant salvation of millions due to their preaching is the reason for the interlude between the sixth and seventh seal.

"After this I beheld , and, lo, a great multitude, which no man could number, of all nations, and

kindred, and people, and tongues, stood before the throne, and before the Lamb, clothed in white robes, and palms in their hands:
And cried with aloud voice, saying, Salvation to our God which sitteth upon the throne, and unto the Lamb." {Rev.7: 9-10}
"And one of the elders answered, saying unto me, Who are these which are arrayed in white robes? And whence came they? {Rev. 7: 13}
This one hundred and forty four thousand represents the remnant of Israel that God preserves down through the centuries.
And I (John) said unto him, Sir, thou knowest. And he said to me, These are they which came out of the Great Tribulation, and have washed their robes, and made them white in the blood of the Lamb," {Rev. 7: 14}
This saving of the one hundred and forty-four thousand and the resultant salvation of millions due to their preaching is the reason for the interlude between the sixth and seventh seal.

Opening the Seventh Seal

The opening of the seventh seal simply announces the blowing of the seven trumpets mentioned previously. But the seventh plague will be so terrible that the denizens of heaven will be silent for half an hour in awe of it. It foreshadows the awful deeds that are to come on the earth. "When he opened the seventh seal, there was silence in heaven for about half an hour" {Rev. 8: 1}

Now we come to the second series of plagues to fall on the earth: the Seven Trumpets. It should be noted that these plagues bear an uncanny resemblance to the ancient plagues Moses called down on Egypt.

The Sounding of the Seven Trumpets
First Trumpet---Trees Burn

"The first angel sounded, and there followed hail and fire mingled with blood. And they were cast upon the earth: and the third part of the trees were burned up, and all the green grass was burnt up." {Rev. 8: 7}

This is to be taken literally. The hail should be taken literally also, but I could not find and information on the significance of the "mingled with blood" phenomenon.

But it should not seem impossible because God rained down burning sulfur on Sodom and Gomorrah.

Second Trumpet---Seas Become Blood

"And the second angel sounded, and as it were a great mountain burning with fire was cast into the sea: and the third part of the sea became blood. And a third part of the creatures which were in the sea, and had life, died; and the third part of the ships were destroyed." {Rev. 8: 8-9}

This should be taken literally. This is the Poseidon adventure multiplied a thousand times or more! The great burning mountain is probably a meteorite or small asteroid from space.

"And the third angel sounded, and there fell a great star from heaven, burning as it were a lamp, and it fell upon a third part of the rivers, and upon the fountains of waters;

And the name of the star is called Wormwood: and a third part of the waters became wormwood; and many men died of the waters, because they were made bitter." {Rev. 8: 10—11}

It is my opinion that the "mountain" of the previous trumpet and this "star" were probably meteorites or asteroids from space.

Fourth Trumpet---Sun, Moon, and Stars Smitten

"And the fourth angel sounded, and the third part of the sun was smitten, and the third part of the moon, and the third part of the stars; so as the third part of them was darkened, and the day shown not for a third part of it, and the night likewise."{Rev. 8: 12}

It is not clear just how this phenomenon operates. Either the heavenly bodies will only be two thirds as bright, or they will shine only two-thirds of the twenty-four hour period. Either way, it doesn't make much difference.

Fifth Trumpet---Fallen Star and Plague of Locusts

"And the fifth angel sounded, and I saw a star fall from heaven unto the earth: and to him was given the key to the bottomless pit." {Rev. 9: 1}
The star is Satan.
"And he opened the bottomless pit; and there arose a smoke out of the pit, as the smoke of a great furnace; and the sun, and the air were darkened by the reason of the smoke of the pit." {Rev. 9: 2}
According to some expositors, this abyss is located between hades, or hell, and paradise. It is the great "gulf fixed" between the rich man (Dives, I believe was his name) in hell and Lazarus in Abraham's

bosom in the parable that Jesus told to his disciples.

The density of this smog-like pollution will make Los Angeles look like a clear, sunny day.

"And there came out of the smoke locusts upon the earth: and unto them was given power, as the scorpions of the earth have power.

And it was commanded that they should not hurt the grass of the earth, neither and green thing; but only those men which have not the seal of God in their foreheads." {Rev. 9: 3-4}

"And to them it was given that they should not kill (the people), but that they should be tormented five months: and their torment was as the torment of a scorpion, when he striketh a man." {Rev. 9: 5}

These locusts are more like bees with a super bad sting than those that just eat the green foliage and grass. Following is an almost unbelievable description of them. The relative sizes of these creatures is not given. They could be very large or about the size of a regular locust.

"And in those days shall men seek death, and shall not find it; and shall flee from them."{Rev. 9: 6}
"And the shapes of the locusts were like unto horses prepared for battle; and their heads were as if it were crowns of gold, and their faces were as the faces of men.

And they had hair as the hair of women, and their teeth were as the teeth of lions.

And they had breastplates, as it were breastplates of iron; and the sound of their wings was as the sound of chariots of many horses running to battle. And they had tails like unto scorpions, and there were stings in their tails: and their power was to hurt men for five months." {Rev. 9: 7-10}

"And they had a king over them, which is the angel of the bottomless pit, whose name in the Hebrew tongue is Abaddon, but in the Greek tongue hath his name Apollyon." {Rev. 9: 11}

At least on expositor says that the locusts are spiritual beings, but still have the ability to inflict pain on mortal men. I do not concur in this interpretation.

This is the first of three woes previously announced. This means the effects of this trumpet and the next two are much more terrible than the other previous trumpets.

Sixth Trumpet---Angels Loosed at River Euphrates

"And the sixth angel sounded, and I heard a voice from the four horns of the golden altar (At God's throne in heaven) which is before God,

Saying to the sixth angel which had the trumpet, Loose the four angels which are bound at the great river Euphrates." {Rev. 9: 13-14}

"And the four angels were loosed, which were prepared for an hour, and a day, and a month, and a year, for to slay the third part of men.

And the number of the army of the horsemen were two hundred thousand thousand: and I heard the number of them." {Rev. 9: 15-16}

"And thus I saw the horses in the vision, and them that sat on them, having breastplates of fire, and of jacinth, and brimstone: and the heads of the horses were as the heads of lions; and out of their mouths issued fire and smoke and brimstone. By these three was the third part of men killed, by the fire, and by the smoke, and by the brimstone, which issued out of their mouths." {Rev. 9: 17-18}

These are unnatural creatures from the underworld. It has been suggested that they are modern-day army tanks. They are demons or demon-controlled. The three plagues mentioned here are literal plagues. This includes the fire, the smoke, and the brimstone. For the hour, day, month and year periods referred to, I have no reference except to say they were well prepared.

"Their power is in their mouth and in their tails: for their tails were like serpents, and had heads. And with them they do hurt." {Rev. 9: 19}

"And the rest of the men which were not killed by these plagues yet repented not." {Rev. 9: 20}

It should be noted that all of these men (people) who are attacked and killed in these catastrophes are those who have refused to repent and accept Christ.

Now we come to the interlude between the sixth and seventh trumpets. By and large, this information in this interlude is to prepare us for the blowing of the seventh trumpet.

"But in the days of the voice of the seventh angel, when he shall begin to sound the mystery for God should be finished, as he hath declared to his servants the prophets" {Rev. 10: 7}

The mystery of God is salvation. This is the mystery of how a holy God could love sinful human beings sufficiently to send his only Son into the world to die for our sins.

Date for the Ending of "The Times of the Gentiles"

"And there was given me a reed like unto a rod: and the angel stood, saying, Rise, and measure the temple of God, and the altar, and them that worship therein.

But the court which is without the temple leave out, and measure it not; for it is given unto the Gentiles: and the holy city shall they tread underfoot forty and two months." {Rev. 11:1-2}

The Temple will be rebuilt in Jerusalem at the beginning of the Tribulation, but it will be nothing like the one that Solomon built.

The presence of this rod means that God is getting ready to deal with the children of Israel. A rod is used for chastisement and judgement. Many people thought that the time of the Gentiles in Jerusalem was ended when Israel captured Jerusalem in the 1967 War. But that has not proven to be the case. This forty and two months corresponds to the last half of the seven year tribulation period.

Duration of the Prophesying of the Two Witnesses

These two witnesses are introduced to us out of the blue, so to speak. We are not given their identity so we can only speculate as to who they will be, and much speculating has certainly been done. There is much agreement on the identity of one of them, that it is Elijah, because it was predicted he would return. (Mal. 4-5), but much controversy over the identity of the second. Even John himself has been suggested as one of these two witnesses because he was the forerunner of Christ at his first coming. Moses is also a primary candidate for various reasons. As best as I can tell, these two witnesses come on the scene sometime near the beginning of the Tribulation. They will have special powers. For example, they will be able to send fire out of their mouths and to kill them that try to persecute them. They also have the power to shut up heaven and keep it from raining. They will be able to bring all kinds of plagues on the earth. They preach the gospel of the kingdom to the whole world. But near the conclusion of the second part of the tribulation, known as the Great Tribulation, the beast from the bottomless pit will be able to kill both of them. It has been suggested that the formation of the one hundred and forty-four thousand saved Jews who preach to the whole world were converted because of the witnessing of these two men. At one time they are believed to be dead, but after three and one half days, they rise to their feet alive again and the whole world sees it and is mystified, terrified and perplexed. The fact that their bodies were allowed to lie three and a half days out in the open street says something about how unfeeling and uncaring and degenerate the people had become by that time.

"And their dead bodies shall lie in the street of the great city, (Jerusalem), which spiritually is called

Sodom and Egypt, where also our Lord was crucified." {Rev. 11: 8}

Sodom means immorality and Egypt stands for materialism both of which had invaded Jerusalem at that time. As a result of the murder of these two witnesses, the people of Jerusalem rejoice and celebrate as though it were a great holiday. As a result, God sends a great earthquake that destroys a tenth part of the city and kills seven thousand people. This results in a mini-revival in Jerusalem for a short period of time.

"And after three days and a half, the Spirit of life from God entered into them, and they stood upon their feet; and a great fear fell upon them which saw them." {Rev. 11: 11}

"And they heard a great voice from heaven saying unto them, Come up hither. And they ascended up to heaven in a cloud; and their enemies beheld them." {Rev. 11: 12}

 This is possible probably through television!

Seventh Trumpet---End of Tribulation and Opening of Temple in Heaven

"And the seventh angel sounded; and there were great voices in heaven, saying, The kingdoms of this world are become the kingdoms of our Loud, and of his Christ; and he shall reign forever and ever." {Rev. 11: 15}

"And the temple of God was opened in heaven, and there were seen in his temple the ark of his testament: And there were lightings, and voices, and thunderings, and an earthquake, and great hail." {Rev. 11: 19}

This opening of the temple in heaven means that God is now dealing with Israel. This declares the prominence of Israel. He is going to keep the covenant he has made with Israel, that a remnant of them will be preserved and have a dominant role among the nations in eternity. The thunderings and lightings indicate that the scene is over. (The concept of a temple in heaven is new to me. I have never heard it mentioned or preached on before.)

The Great Tribulation Begins
Seven Performers during the Great Tribulation
"And there appeared a great wonder in heaven; a woman clothed with the sun, and the moon under her feet, and upon her head a crown of twelve stars: And she being great with child, travailing in birth and pained to be delivered." {Rev. 12: 1—2} The woman is the nation of Israel and the child is Jesus. They are both symbolic.

"And there appeared another wonder in heaven; and behold a great red dragon, having seven heads and ten horns, and seven crowns upon his heads. And his tail drew a third part of the stars of heaven, and did cast them to the earth: and the dragon stood before the woman which was ready to be delivered, for to devour her child as soon as it was born." {Rev. 12: 3-4}

The red dragon is Satan and he was cast out of heaven with a third of the angels when he makes war with Michael and the other angels. He can no longer go there to accuse the people on earth who are saved as he has throughout the centuries. This occurs about the Beginning of the Great Tribulation. He is called great because of his vast power, and "red" because he was a murderer from the beginning. He was called Dragon because of the viciousness of his character. (However, at least one famous expositor maintains that this casting out of Satan from heaven refers to the original casting out in the Old Testament.) "Seven heads" suggest the perfection of wisdom and the ten horns suggest the final division of the Roman Empire. The dragon hates the Man Child because it was predicted from the beginning that the child would be the undoing of Satan.

"And she brought forth a man child (Christ) who was to rule all the nations with a rod of iron: and her child was caught up unto God, and to his throne.

And the woman (Israel) fled into the wilderness, where she hath a place prepared of God, that they should feed her there a thousand two hundred and three score days." {Rev. 12: 5-6}

Some expositors believe this wilderness to be the ancient city of Petra with its myriad of underground tunnels and chambers.

"And there was war in heaven: Michael and his angels fought against the dragon: and the dragon fought and his angels,

And prevailed not; neither was their place found anymore in heaven.

And the great dragon was cast out, that old serpent, called the Devil, and Satan, which deceiveth the whole world: he was cast out into the earth, and his angels were cast out with him." {Rev. 12: 7-9}

Believe it or not, there was war in heaven for a second time. Up until this time Satan has had access to heaven because the Bible says that he went there often to accuse the brethren to God. But now he is cast out and cannot even do that anymore. But now that he is on earth fulltime, he is more of a threat to man than ever before.

"And I heard a loud voice saying in heaven, Now is come salvation, and strength, and the kingdom of our God, and the power of Christ: for the accuser of our brethren is cast down, which accused them before our God day and night.

And they overcame him by the blood of the Lamb, and by the word of their testimony: and they loved not their lives unto death.

Therefore rejoice, ye heavens, and ye that dwell in them. Woe to the inhabitants of the earth and of the sea! for the devil is come down unto you, having great wrath, because he knoweth that he hath but a short time." {Rev. 12: 10-12}

This is where Satan (indwelling the Antichrist) began his movement to take over political power over the whole world.

"And when the dragon saw that he was cast unto the earth, he persecuted the woman which brought forth the man child.

And to the woman was given two wings of a great eagle that she might fly into the wilderness, into her place, where she is nourished for a time, and times and half a time from the face of the serpent." {Rev. 12: 13-14}

The image of an eagle is not something that the people of Israel would not readily identify with because of its use in earlier writings of the Old Testament. For example, it is associated with their escape from Egypt, e.g. God brought them out on the wings of eagles.

"And the serpent cast out of his mouth water as a flood after the woman, that he might cause her to be carried away of the flood.

And the earth helped the woman, and the earth opened her mouth, and swallowed up the flood which the dragon cast out of his mouth." {Rev. 12: 15-16}

This is to be interpreted literally. If God could open up the earth like he did when the children of Israel worshiped the golden calf in the Old

Testament and swallowed them up, he can cause the earth to soak up this flood of water!

Wild Beast Out of the Sea---Description, a Political Power and a Person

"And I stood upon the sand of the sea, and saw a great beast rise up out of the sea, having seven heads and ten horns, and upon his horns ten crowns, and upon his head the name of blasphemy." {Rev. 13: 1}

The beast is the Antichrist who comes from the people of the nations represented by the sea. It is believed by some expositors that this sea refers to the Mediterranean Sea and the lands around it. To make a long story short, it is believe by some that the nationality of the Antichrist is a mixture of Roman-Grecian Jew, and that he will rise up out of one of the lands touching the Mediterranean Sea. Thus, he is a composite man representing all the peoples of the earth. The ten horns are the nations that make up the revived Roman Empire. The ten crowns represent the rulers (kings) of these ten countries. This scripture refers to the fact that the Antichrist will become the supreme ruler of the earth sometime around the beginning of the Great Tribulation. He will be able to do this because of his political acumen and his powerful personality. He will also become the supreme authority of the apostate church which has joined and combined with all the religions of the world into one world-wide Church. The Antichrist manages to get control of this one world church about the same time that he becomes the world ruler. The rulers of the earth will give their armies to the Antichrist and also their economic power. Both of these takeovers occur at the beginning of the Great Tribulation. The leaders of the countries will come to the conclusion that they cannot keep peace among themselves and will voluntarily give this power to the one man rule of the Antichrist. The Antichrist will be given control of the world economy about this time also. The False Prophet comes from Israel, and is instrumental in the rise of the Antichrist and his takeover of the world church. The False Prophet is like a mouthpiece, a lawyer, a spokesperson, for the Antichrist.

And the beast which I saw was like unto a leopard, and his feet were like the feet of a bear, and his mouth was like the mouth of a lion: and the dragon gave him his power, and his seat, and great authority." [Rev. 13: 2]

This means that the Antichrist combines the power of four representative kingdoms that Daniel saw in his vision. Three of these are the Graeco-Macedonia, Media-Persia, and Babylon. The fourth is yet to come.

"And I saw one of its heads as it were to death; and his deadly wound was healed: and all the world wondered after the beast." {Rev." 13: 3}

Only God has the power to raise the dead. This was, almost certainly, a false, fake resurrection engineered by Satan. Jesus was raised from the dead and it appears that the Antichrist is also. This is one of the ways the Antichrist hopes to deceive men. He tries to be as close to like Jesus as he can be in order to deceive people. Now Satan is indwelling the Antichrist and performs miracle after miracle.

"And I beheld another beast coming up from out of the earth; and he had two horns like a lamb, and he spake as a dragon." {Rev. 13: 11}

This is the False Prophet who is primarily a religious leader. The note that he came out of the earth means that he probably came out of the nation of Israel. The horns denote authority and the fact that he appears as a lamb denotes deception. This False Prophet will be equipped by Satan to do signs and wonders and all sorts of miracles, even the power to call down fire from heaven, all to deceive the people to accept the Antichrist.

This is the False Prophet.

It was near the beginning of the takeover of the church at the beginning of the Great Tribulation

that the Antichrist had a huge statue of his likeness
set up in the temple with the aid of the False
Prophet and forced the world to worship it. He
even could even make it talk. He sets himself up
in the temple and declares himself to be God.

"And he had power to give life unto the image of
the beast that the image of the beast should both
speak, and cause that as many as would not
worship the beast should be killed.

And he causeth all, both small and great, rich and
poor, free and bond, to receive a mark in their right
hand, or in their foreheads:

And that no man might buy or sell, save he that
had the mark, or the name of the beast, or the
number of his name." {Rev. 13: 15-17}

One reason for this probably was the shortage of
food. Another reason, I believe, was for control of
the masses.

"Here is wisdom. Let him that hath understanding
count the number of the beast: for it is the number

of a man; and his number is Six hundred threescore and six." {Rev. 13: 18}

The End of the Great Tribulation

Judgment on those with the Mark of the Beast
"And the third angel followed them, saying with a loud voice, If any man worship the beast and his image, and receive his mark in his forehead or in his hand,
The same shall drink of the wine of the wrath of God, which is poured out without mixture into the cup of his indignation; and he shall be tormented with fire and brimstone in the presence of the holy angels, and in the presence of the Lamb;
And the smoke of their torment ascendeth up for ever and ever: and they have no rest day or night, who worship the beast and his image, and whosoever receiveth the mark of his name." {Rev. 14: 9}

The Coming of Armageddon

"And I looked, and behold a white cloud, and upon the cloud one sat like unto the Son of man, (Jesus Christ) having on his head a golden crown, and in his hand a sharp sickle." {Rev. 14: 14}

The sharp sickle indicates judgment.

"And the angel thrust in his sickle into the earth, and gathered the vine of the earth, and cast it into the great winepress of the wrath of God.

And the winepress was trodden without the city, and blood came out of the winepress, even unto the horse bridles, by the space of a thousand and six hundred furlongs. {Rev. 14: 19-20}

This is a distance of about 185 miles. This is the scene after the Battle of Armageddon. Blood up to a horse's bridle is about four feet. One expositor says this is more of a war that lasts several months than just one battle. Two other preceding battles to that of Armageddon some expositors say are the Battle of Jehoshaphat and the Battle of Jerusalem. These occur at the end of the Great Tribulation when Jesus and all the hosts of heaven return to earth.

(One explanation for the four feet of blood is that it will be a mixture of blood and water melted from the gigantic chunks of hail.)

The Seven Bowls of Wrath

The pouring out of the seven bowls of wrath covers the entire forty-two months of the second half of the seven year period, and is known as the Great Tribulation.

"And after this, I looked, and, behold, the temple of the tabernacle of the testimony in heaven was opened:

And the seven angels came out of the temple, having the seven plagues, clothed in pure and white linen, and having their breasts girded with golden girdles." {Rev. 15: 5-6}

And one of the four beasts gave unto the seven angels seven golden vials full of the wrath of God, who liveth forever and ever.

And the temple was filled with smoke from the glory of God, and from his power; and no man was able to enter into the temple till the seven plagues of the seven angels were fulfilled." {Rev. 15: 7-8}

Pouring Out of the Seven Vials

"And I heard a great voice out of the temple saying to the seven angels, Go your ways, and pour out the vials of the wrath of God upon the earth." {Rev. 16: 1}

Pouring Out of the First Vial

"And the first went, and poured out his vial upon the earth; and there fell a noisome and grievous sore upon the men which had the mark of the beast, and upon them who had worshiped his image." {Rev. 16: 2}

This judgment of the sores is for those who have received the mark of the beast to try to get them to repent, but they continue to rebel against Christ. Yes, it is believed by some expositors that these sores only afflict the people who have the mark of the beast.

Pouring Out of the Second Vial

"And the second angel poured out his vial on the sea; and it became as the blood of a dead man: and every living soul died in the sea. {Rev. 16: 3} The stench was horrific because of the sea creatures that were dead floating on the surface and lining the shore. There is no more commerce, and human beings died like flies. Still there was no repentance of mankind. The rest of these plagues, it seems to me, has to affect all those people who did not have the mark of the beast also.

Pouring Out of the Third Vial

"And the third angel poured out his vial upon the rivers and fountains of waters; and they became blood.

And I heard the angel of the waters say, Thou art righteous, O Lord. Which art, and wast, and shall be, because thou hast judged thus,

For they have shed the blood of saints and prophets, and thou hast given them blood to drink, for they are worthy.

And I heard another out of the altar say, Even so, Lord God Almighty, true and righteous are thy judgments." {Rev. 16: 4-7}

The total water supply of the earth will be cut off which will result in an unparalleled loss of life. The altar refers to the altar of the Saints in heaven praying for justice to be fulfilled. But they were told to wait a little while longer and justice would be done.

Pouring Out of the Fourth Vial

"And the fourth angel poured out his vial upon the sun, and power was given to him to scorch men with fire.

And men were scorched with great heat, and blasphemed the name of God, which hath power over these plagues: and they repented not to give him glory." {Rev. 16: 8-9}

When the earth gets as little as two degrees closer to the sun the heat increases greatly. This is probably what God does with the sun here.

Pouring Out of the Fifth Vial

"And the fifth angel poured out his vial upon the seat of the beast; and his kingdom was full of darkness; and thy gnawed their tongues for pain. And blasphemed the God of heaven because of their pains and sores, and repented not of their deeds." {Rev. 16: 10-11}

Ever bitten your tongue? How painful it was! Here men will actually be gnawing their tongues because of terrible pain. But men still refused to repent.

Pouring Out of the Sixth Vial

"And the sixth angel poured out his vial upon the great fiver Euphrates; and the water there of was dried up, that the way of the kings of the east might be prepared." {Rev. 16: 12}

This drying up of the Euphrates River is to prepare the way for the two hundred million man army of the kings of the east coming for the Battle of Armageddon. This was written in a time when the entire population of the world was only a few million people. Up until only a couple of centuries ago has it become possible for the kings of the east to have a two hundred million man army. Who could have foreseen that the population of India and China alone would today be four billion plus. They are easily able to field a two hundred million man army today. For the people who read these words before about the 1850s before the population explosion must have wondered how this would be possible.

Interlude: Kings of the Earth Proceed to the Battle of Armageddon

The war and/or the battle occurs just before the end of the Great Tribulation. (Remember that the first half of the seven year period is known as the Tribulation and the second half is known as the Great Tribulation.)

"And I saw three unclean spirits like frogs come of the mouth of the dragon, and out of the mouth of the beast, and out of the mouth of the false prophet.

For they are the spirits of devils, working miracles, which go fourth unto the kings of the earth and of the whole world to gather them to the battle of the great day of God Almighty." {Rev. 16: 13-14}

 This will occur about the middle of the Great Tribulation, so say some expositors, but I believe it will be closer to the end of the Great Tribulation. The reason for their position is they believe the battle of Armageddon is more like an extensive war. Satan, the Antichrist, and the False Prophet are all together in this mighty movement. The frogs are to be taken as symbols, not literally. This evil trinity will convince the nations of the world to join them in this undertaking.

"And he gathered them together into a place called in the Hebrew tongue Armageddon." {Rev. 16: 16}

Some expositors say there will be four battles. The actual culminating battle, called Armageddon, occurs very near the end of the Great Tribulation. Two of these battles before the Battle of Armageddon are the Battle of Megiddo Valley and the Battle of Jerusalem, both of which the forces of Christ win.

Napoleon is supposed to have said that this site is the most perfect place for a huge battle in the entire world.

Pouring Out of the Seventh Vial

"And the seventh angel poured out his vial into the air; and there came a great voice out of the temple of heaven, from the throne, saying, It is done. This marks the end of the Great Tribulation. And there were voices, and thunders, and lightings, and there was a great earthquake, such as not since men were upon the earth, so mighty an earthquake, and so great. {Rev. 16: 17-18}

"And the great city was divided into three parts, and the cities of the nations fell: and great Babylon came into remembrance before God, to give unto her the cup of wine of the fierceness of his wrath. And every island fled away, and the mountains were not found,

And there fell upon men great hail out of heaven, every stone about the weight of a talent: (about one hundred and thirty-five pounds) and men blasphemed God because of the plague of hail; for the plague thereof was exceeding great." {Rev. 16: 19-21}

Even the islands were moved out of their places, and the mountains were moved about, so fierce was this earthquake. And the great cities of the world like New York and Tokyo and Mexico City were shaken and destroyed. The terrible hailstorm ends the Great Tribulation period. (Remember the "Tribulation" refers to the first three and one half years of the seven year period, and the "Great Tribulation" refers to the second half of this seven year period.) It is estimated that over two billion people will die during this seven year period, and this is a conservative estimate. This is about one-half, or fifty percent, of the population of the earth during this time.

The Apostate Church during the Great Tribulation

"And there came one if the seven angels which had the seven vials, and talked with me, saying, come hither; I will show thee the judgment of the great whore that sitteth upon many waters.

Whom the kings of the earth have committed fornication (have made unholy agreements with her for personal and financial gain,) and the inhabitants of the earth have been made drunk with the wine of her fornication." {Rev. 17: 1-2}

The great harlot is the false church and the wild beast is the restored Roman Empire.

"So he carried me away in the spirit into the wilderness: and I saw a woman sit upon a scarlet colored beast, full of names of blasphemy, having seven heads and ten horns." {Rev. 17: 3}

 (In some scripture not quoted here we see a little horn rise up from the ten horns. This represents the Antichrist who first subdues three of the larger horns-nations-, then he takes over the other seven horns. Thus he became the ruler of the revived Roman Empire.)

The wilderness is literal, and corresponds to the wilderness around Rome and Babylon. The seven hills refers to where Rome is located. The wild beast is the Antichrist. The ten horns are ten kings who rule over the ten nations of the revived Roman Empire. The woman is a false religious system. The Antichrist has taken control of this false religious system with the aid of the False Prophet. This takeover has occurred sometime during the first part of the first half of the seven year period. It is finally destroyed by the Antichrist, making way for the worship of the Antichrist by the entire world at the end of the first three and one half years of the Tribulation.

The Judgement of Commercial and Political Babylon

"And after these things I saw another angel come down from heaven having great power; and the earth was lightened with his glory." {Rev. 18: 1} "And he cried mightily with a strong voice, saying, Babylon the great is fallen, is fallen, and has become the habitation of devils, and the hold of every foul spirit. And a cage of every unclean and hateful bird. {Rev. 18: 2}

Babylon has become the center of the commercial activity during the Great Tribulation. It has replaced New York and Beijing and London.

"Therefore shall her plagues come in one day, death, and mourning, and famine; and she shall be utterly burned with fire: for strong is the Lord God who judgeth her." {Rev. 18: 8}

"And the kings (and merchants) of the earth, who have committed fornication and lived deliciously with her, (made unholy alliances for financial gain) shall bewail her, and lament for her, when they shall see the smoke of her burning." {Rev. 18: 9} This destruction of Babylon shall all take place in one hour, and it shall be by fire. It is said that the entire area beneath Babylon is a layer of tar. Some speculate that this tar burning is the fire that destroys Babylon.

"And a mighty angel took up a stone like a great millstone, and cast it into the sea, saying, Thus with violence shall the great city Babylon be

thrown down, and shall be found no more at all."
{Rev. 18: 21}

No reference is made concerning the authenticity of the millstone, but I believe it should be taken literally. It represents the suddenness and complete destruction of the city. It is, no doubt, an object from space, such as a huge meteorite. But, as we have already seen, her destruction has been by earthquakes, famine, plagues, and fire.

"And in her was found the blood of the prophets, and of saints, and of all that were slain upon the earth." {Rev. 18: 24}

These are those who were persecuted in the city throughout the Great Tribulation Period. The positive side of all this violence and destruction is the Day of the Lord, the Millennium, or thousand years is being ushered in. As Babylon is the economic and commercial capital of the world during the Great Tribulation, so is Jerusalem the capital of the religious world. (The Antichrist will have begun in Rome, and the False Prophet will have begun in Jerusalem.)

Marriage and Marriage Supper of the Lamb and the Return of Christ in Judgement

To begin this section, let me say there is much difference of opinion as to the actual makeup of the people at the marriage supper of the Lamb. "After these things I heard a great voice of much people in heaven, saying, Alleluia; Salvation, and glory, and honor, and power, unto the Lord our God." {Rev. 19: 1} Let us be glad and rejoice, and give honor to him: for the marriage of the Lamb is come, and his wife hath made herself ready. And to her was granted that she should be arrayed in fine linen, clean and white: for the fine linen is the righteousness of saints." {Rev. 19: 7-8} This is the time come for the marriage of the Lamb. It takes place in heaven during the seven years of tribulation here on earth. His bride is the called-out church and no one else. Not even the

Old Testament saints will be there. The fine linen represents the righteous acts of the saints, and the wedding gown is the righteous acts of the church. "And he saith unto me, Write, Blessed are they which are called to the marriage supper of the Lamb. And he saith unto me, These are the true sayings of God." {Rev. 19: 9}

As I said earlier, there is much disagreement as to who all will actually be at the marriage supper of the Lamb. Some say that even the bride will not be there. I believe those who say the bride, the church, will be there along with the Old Testament saints and the saved out of the seven year tribulation. But we will understand it better by and by.

The wedding of the Lamb to his bride the church takes place in heaven, and the marriage supper of the Lamb takes place on earth, most likely, according to some expositors, in Jerusalem at the end of the Great Tribulation when Jesus returns to the earth with the Church and the saints in heaven.

However, some commentators say the marriage supper will be in heaven. I am of this persuasion.

Return of Christ to the Earth as King of Kings and Lord of Lords

This occurs at the end of the seven years. (At the end of the Great Tribulation and before the Millennial Kingdom.)

"And I saw the heaven opened, and behold a white horse; and he that sat upon him was called Faithful and True, in righteousness he doth judge and make war.

His eyes were as a flame of fire, and on his head were many crowns; and he had a name written, that no man knew, but he himself." {Rev. 19: 11-12}

He is called Faithful and True because he has come to do what he has planned before the begining of time, and because he is true. He has come to judge and make war. He is going to rule the earth as a dictator with a rod of iron during the Millennial Reign.

"And he was clothed with a vesture dipped in blood: and his name is called the Word of God.

The armies which were in heaven followed him on white horses, clothed in fine linen, white and clean.

And out of his mouth goeth a sharp sword, that with it he should subdue the nations, and he shall rule them with a rod of iron; he treadeth the winepress of the fierceness and wrath of Almighty God.

And he hath on his vesture and on his thigh a name written, KING OF KINGS AND LORD OF LORDS." {Rev. 13: 16}

The armies in heaven are evidently the legions of angels that do his bidding. Many expositors believe the church will also be in this army as well as the Old Testament saints and the saved out of the Tribulation and Great Tribulation. I am of this persuasion.

"And I saw an angel standing in the sun; and he cried with a loud voice, saying to all the fouls that fly in the midst of heaven, Come and gather yourselves together unto the supper of the great God.

That ye may eat the flesh of kings, and the flesh of captains, and the flesh of mighty men, and the flesh of horses, and of them that sit on them, and the flesh of all men, both free and bond, both small and great." {Rev. 19: 17-18}

This is an indication of the total destruction of the evil armies and an invitation to the birds to feast on the flesh of the dead. Now hell is opened up for the first time. Remember, it is Jesus who will do the actual fighting with the sword-words-that proceed out of his mouth.

"And I saw the beast, and the kings of the earth, and their armies, gathered together to make war against him that sat on the horse, and against the army.

And the beast was taken, and with him the false prophet that wrought miracles before him, with guile he deceived them that had received the mark of the beast, and them that worshiped his image. They both were cast alive into the lake of fire burning with brimstone.

And the remnant were slain with the sword of him that sat upon the horse, which sword proceeded out of his mouth: and all of the fowls were filled with their flesh." {Rev. 19: 19-21}

The lake of fire should be taken as literal, but the sword out of Christ's mouth is his words. These are the first two to be cast into hell. The Devil hasn't been put there yet.

"And I saw and angel come down from heaven, having the key of the bottomless pit and a great chain in his hand.

And he laid hold on the dragon, that old serpent, which is the Devil, and Satan, and bound him a thousand years. {Rev. 20: 2}

I once had a preacher friend who said the only thing he wanted to do at this time was to ask God to let him carry the chain that the angel would use to bind the dragon to confine him in the bottomless pit!

And cast him into the bottomless pit, and shut him up, and set a seal upon him, that he should deceive the nations no more, till the thousand years be fulfilled: After that he must be loosed a little season." {Rev. 20:1-3}

The Devil's power has been so reduced that an angel has the strength to lock him up. Then, now, begins the thousand year Millennial Reign.

"And I saw thrones, and they that sat upon them, and judgment was given unto them: and I saw the souls of them that were beheaded for the witness of Jesus, and for the word of God, and which had not worshiped the beast, neither his image, neither had received his mark upon their foreheads, or in their hands; and they lived and reigned with Christ a thousand years."

It is believed by some that some of the church will be given specific tasks to perform during this thousand years, such as rule over cities. It is believed by some expositors that the remnant of the Jews, the one hundred and forty-four thousand, will also have a part in this thousand year reign. The saved still on the earth at the end of the Great Tribulation will also have entered the Millennial Kingdom and will have had children, thus helping to populate the earth during that time.

These will be the people that Satan will try to deceive at the end of the thousand years when he is released out of the bottomless pit for a little season. The time of the Millennial Kingdom is the time of the new heaven and sew earth so created at the beginning of the thousand year period by fire. (Some expositors believe the new heaven and new earth will be created at the end of the thousand year Millennial Reign. I do not concur.) There will be no more sea and the barren places such as the former deserts will bloom as a rose. It will be the era when the lion shall lie down with the Lamb. There will be no more war, and diseases will be unheard of. There will be no more dying among the people of God, and some will live a thousand years. We are going to have glorified bodies and can travel unhindered by physical objects. Christ will sit in power in Jerusalem and rule the nations with a rod of iron. It is truly going to be heaven on earth.

One expositor insist that people born of those who entered the Kingdom in fleshly bodies from the Great Tribulation will live only one hundred years, if they do not trust Christ as their savior. (This is a concept with which I have not been familiar with before beginning research for this book. And I am not sure I agree with it. If this is the case, there will be relatively few people living at the end of the thousand year reign who have not accepted Christ to be deceive by Satan in his little season. Furthermore, I cannot find any scripture for it.)

But the rest of the dead lived not again until the thousand years were finished. This is the first resurrection." {Rev. 20: 4}

These are the dead who died without Christ throughout the Old Testament years and the Church Age and the seven year period of tribulations.

"And when the thousand years are expired, Satan shall be loosed out of his prison,

And shall go out to deceive the nations which are in the four quarters of the earth, Gog and Magog, to gather together to battle: the number of whom is as the sand of the sea.

(There will be millions of people born during the Millennial Reign and they get a chance to choose Christ over the devil for a little season.)

And they went up on the breath of the earth, and compassed the camp of the saints about, and the beloved city: and fire came down from God out of heaven, and devoured them." {Rev. 20: 7-9}

This is the last rebellion of Satan and man against God. The beloved city is Jerusalem.

"And the devil that deceived them (of the thousand year reign) was cast into the lake of fire and brimstone, where the beast and the false prophet are, and shall be tormented day and night forever and ever." {Rev. 20: 10}

Great White Throne Judgement

"And I saw a great white throne, and him that sat on it, from whose face the heaven and earth fled away; and there was no place found for them." {Rev. 20: 1}

This judgment takes place at the end of the thousand year reign.

All the lost of all the ages will be judged there, those previously mentioned as well as those who were deceived by Satan who rejected Christ during the Millennial Reign.

"And I saw the dead, small and great, stand before God; and the books were opened: and another book was opened, which is the book of life: and the dead were judged out of those things which were written in the books, according to their works.

And the sea gave up the dead which were in it; and death and hell delivered up the dead which were in them: and they were judged every man according to their works." {Rev. 20: 12-13}

They are all lost because their names were not written in the Book of Life. Their names had been blotted out when they refused to accept Christ. There is the Book of Life in which every person who is born has their name recorded in it. As they die without receiving Christ, their names are blotted out of it. When people receive Christ, their names are written in the Lamb's Book of Life and is never blotted out.

"And death and hell were cast into the lake of fie. This is the second death. And whosoever was not found written in the book of life were cast into the lake of fire." {Rev. 20: 14-15}

Just before they are cast into the lake of fire, every soul that has rejected Christ will be required to bow their knee and worship God the Father, the Son, and the Holy Spirit.

At the Great White Throne all of the lost of all the ages receive a fair trial and all are found guilty. I believe there are degrees in hell just as people in heaven will not be rewarded equally because of their works. The Bible says that some will be beaten with many stripes and some with few.

"And that servant, which knew not his Lord's will. And prepared not himself, neither did according to his will, shall be beaten with many stripes.

But he that knew not, and did commit things worthy of stripes, shall be beaten with few stripes. For unto whomsoever much is given, of him shall much be required: and to whom men have committed much, of him they will ask the more."
{Luke 12: 47-48]

Also, God is a just God. That is the reason for this judgement, to assign the lost their appropriate place based on their works. I believe Hitler and Stalin and such people as they were, will be in the lowest regions of hell. And a young person who has just reached the age of accountability, but has not yet accepted Christ, will not be punished as severely as other people who have lived a long, evil, Christ-rejecting life.

New Jerusalem, the Eternal Abode of the Church

The rest of Revelation deals with the new heaven and new earth and the saved's eternal existence in it. Its beauty and shape is described among other attributes. I encourage the reader to review it at his/her leisure. Mostly it is self-explanatory, and most people are familiar with it because it has been the subject of many sermons down through the years. One simply has to be able to visualize it in order to grasp the magnificence of it. Following is a brief description of it.

"And there came unto me one of the seven angels, which had the seven vials full of seven last plagues, and talked with me, saying, Come hither, and I will show thee the bride, the Lamb's wife. {Rev. 21: 9}

Having the glory of God: and her light was like unto a stone most precious, even like a jasper stone, clear as crystal {Rev 21: 11}.

And had a wall great and high, and had twelve gates, and the gates twelve angels, and names written thereon, which are the names of the twelve tribes of the children of Israel: On the east three gates, on the north three gates: on the south three gates: and on the west three gates {Rev 21:12-13}.

And the wall of the city had twelve foundations, and in them the names of the twelve apostles of the Lamb {{Rev.21 14}.

And the city lieth foursquare, and the length iis as large as the breath: And he measureth the city with the reed, twelve thousand furlongs. The length and the breath and the height of it are equal {Rev, 21: 15-16}.

And he measured the wall thereof, an hundred and forty cubits, according to the measure of a man, that is, of the angel.

And the building of the wall of it was jasper: and the city was pure gold, like unto cleat glass {Rev. 21: 17-18}.

And the foundations of the wall of the city were garnished with all manner of precious stones. {Rev. 21: 19}.

And the twelve gates were twelve pearls: every several gate was on one pearl: and the street of the city was pure gold, as it were transparent glass {Rev. 21 21}.

…and the lamb is the light thereof." {Rev. 21: 22} It is believed that the city will be a cube fifteen hundred miles square and would reach from the east coast to the Mississippi river and from the Canadian border to the Gulf of Mexico and be fifteen hundred miles high! It is said to be able to

house twenty billion people with each one having a
block space of one cubic mile!

(Some expositors believe the heavenly city, New
Jerusalem, will come to the earth. Others believe
it will be suspended in the air above the surface on
the earth, and we will be able to travel from the
earth to the heavenly city at will. Israel and the
other nations will travel up there periodically to
worship God.)

Final Invitation and Warning

"And the Spirit and the bride say, Come, And let
him that hearth say, Come, And let him that is
athirst come, And whosoever will, let him; take the
water of life freely.

For I testify unto every man that heareth the
prophesy of this book, If any man shall add unto
these things, God shall add unto him the plagues
that are written in this book:

And if any man shall take away from the words of
the book of this prophesy, God shall take away his

part out of the book of life, and out of the holy city, and from the things that are written in this book." {Rev. 22: 17-19.}

This is an invitation to Christ to come as well as to sinners. This is a dire warning to anyone that tampers with this book. And there are lots of people who have "taken out," that don't believe parts of this book.

Final Promise and Prayer

"He which testifieth these things saith, Surely I come quickly. Amen. Even so, come, Lord Jesus. The grace of our Lord Jesus Christ be with you all. Amen."{Rev. 22: 20-21}

The Old Testament ends with a curse, and the New Testament ends with a benediction of grace to all. God is still extending his grace to all, especially to the unsaved.

This seems to be an appropriate place to end this treatise.

Credits

No Fear of the Storm

Tim LaHaye

Multnomah Press Books, 1992

Revelation Unveiled

Tim Lahaye

Zondervan Publishing House, 1999

Through the Bible with J. Vernon McGee Volume

V 1Corinthians-Revelation

J. Vernon McGee

Thomas Nelson Publishers, 1983

King James Version, Scofield Bible

Epilogue

Although the actual writing of this book was a pleasure, I did find it more challenging than I anticipated. I discovered that easy-to-read, understandable, reference sources were not easy to find. I rechecked my work many times for accuracy and clearness. I made many trips from my desk to the computer to change, add to, or take away from what I had written. As a result, I believe I have a book that the average layman will find useful.

Dr. Larry G. Morgan

Postscript

I have worked hard on this book, and if any praise comes to, I can only give God the glory. While I have been writing it, I have labored under a mental and emotional burden. I am waiting for the results of some clinical tests I am afraid will give me some bad news about my physical condition and future. I have never done much, if anything, for the Lord, but I hope this book will count for something along that line, and perhaps I can live to accomplish a little more for Him.

Dr. Larry G. Morgan

Post Postscript

People have often struggled with the dilemma of where evil came from. I have finally found an answer, albeit it tenuous. In a nutshell, it was created by Satan out of good forces that God created. By misapplying them and manipulating them, he manufactured evil out of good. To illustrate this we can use the chemical world. It is possible to take one element by itself and it is harmless, perhaps even beneficial, to people. But when combined with a certain other element, or elements, it becomes a deadly poison. One example is common salt. Separate its two elements which are combined to create salt, sodium and chlorine, and the result is two deadly poisons. This is analogous to what it is said by some, how evil was created.

Other Books by Dr. Larry G. Morgan

Ivy

Mountain Born, Mountain Molded

Appalachian Mountain Memories

Golf Poems for Everyone

Old Time Religion in the Southern Appalachians

Strange Life-Struggling with the Mysteries of OCD

Joseph' Son

The Journey

A Timeline for Creation and other Essays

A Peculiar People-The Melungeons